Swedish Traditions

51 classic dishes

Christer Lingström
Lennart Häger
Photos: Bruno Ehrs

English translation: Melody Favish

Swedish traditions

Why does it seem completely wrong if there is no herring at Midsummer and no ham on the Christmas buffet? How can you celebrate a crayfish feast without those colorful little hats? And why are certain traditions never meant to be broken?

This book is about our most important festive tables. About evenings that strengthen our roots and family ties, and about rituals that give newcomers to Sweden their first exotic taste of our culture.

Christer Lingström of Edsbacka Krog is a true traditionalist. As a traveling ambassador for Swedish food, with a passion for crayfish and Lenten buns, he teaches the rest of the world how the most Swedish of dishes should taste. And now he is doing that in book form.

"According to tradition" is something we often say. Without really knowing why. This book tells of holidays and special days that we have celebrated for hundreds of years and will continue to celebrate as long as we pass the traditions on to future generations.

By serving the most popular Swedish festive dishes, you are preserving our traditions for posterity.

This year, too.

Note: When preparing these recipes, use either deciliters or cups (in parentheses). Do not combine the two types of measurement in the same recipe.

Seven kinds of cookies

Sju sorters kakor

No Swedish coffee klatch is complete without seven kinds of cookies. This custom started in the 1800s, when drinking coffee once again was permitted after it had been forbidden for a time. Cookie and cake recipes became very popular. Some say the reason for so many kinds of cookies on the platter has to do with hostesses trying to outdo one another.

Mocha mousse

Kaffemousse

The Swedes are a coffee-drinking people, and a meal without coffee seems incomplete. In this recipe, which dates from the 1850s, coffee is used in a mousse.

6–8 SERVINGS

1 DL (1/2 CUP) SUGAR
3 EGG YOLKS
1/2 DL (1/4 CUP) STRONG COFFEE
260 G (9 OUNCES) MILK CHOCOLATE, MELTED
4 DL (1 2/3 CUPS) WHIPPING CREAM

Whisk sugar, egg yolks and coffee in a saucepan over medium heat until the mixture begins to thicken. The temperature will be around 80 °C (175 °F). Beat in the chocolate, mixing well. Let cool a little. Whip the cream and fold lightly but thoroughly into the chocolate mixture. Pour into coffee cups and refrigerate for 2 hours.

Serve with arrak sauce.

Arrak sauce:
6–8 SERVINGS

2 1/2 DL (1 CUP) LIGHT CREAM
5 EGG YOLKS
2–3 TABLESPOONS SUGAR
1 DL (1/2 CUP) ARRAK

Heat the cream to boiling. Let cool. Beat egg yolks and sugar with an electric mixer until light and fluffy. Stir in the arrak. Whisk the arrak mixture into the cream. Reheat, whisking constantly, until it begins to thicken and is creamy like vanilla custard. Do not allow to boil or the eggs will scramble. Remove from the heat and whisk occasionally while cooling. Serve slightly warm with the cold mousse.

Note: Swedish Punsch liqueur can be used instead of arrak.

Jam slices

Syltkakor

AROUND 50 COOKIES

200 G (7 OUNCES) SOFT BUTTER
1 TEASPOON VANILLA SUGAR OR
    1/2 TEASPOON VANILLA EXTRACT
1 DL (1/2 CUP) SUGAR
4 1/2–5 DL (1 3/4–2 CUPS) ALL-PURPOSE FLOUR
RASPBERRY PRESERVES, STRAINED
    (WITHOUT LARGE PIECES OF FRUIT)

Preheat the oven to 175 °C (350 °F). Beat butter, vanilla sugar and sugar until light and fluffy with an electric mixer. Add flour and beat at low speed until crumbly. Gather the dough and press together. Divide into 3–4 equal parts.

Roll each piece of dough into a log and place on a baking sheet lined with baking parchment. Lightly press down each log and make a groove down the center. Spoon a thin layer of red preserves, preferably raspberry, down the center of each length. This is easy if you buy it in a plastic squeeze container.

Bake in the center of the oven for 10–12 minutes, until lightly golden. While still warm, cut on the diagonal into slices. It is also possible to make separate cookies. Roll the dough into small balls and place on a parchment-lined baking sheet. Make an indentation with your finger in each ball and place a small spoonful of preserves in the center. Bake for 8–10 minutes.

Let cool on the baking sheet or pull the parchment off the baking sheet onto the kitchen countertop.

Cat tongues

Katt-tungor

AROUND 20 COOKIES

50 G (3 1/2 TABLESPOONS) SOFT BUTTER
3 1/2 TABLESPOONS SUGAR
1 EGG
5 TABLESPOONS (1/3 CUP) ALL-PURPOSE
    FLOUR
SLICED ALMONDS

Preheat the oven to 170°C (350°F).
Beat butter and sugar until light and
fluffy. Add the egg, beating well. Stir
in the flour, combining well. Spoon into
a cookie press or pastry bag with a
small opening. Press lengths onto
a baking sheet lined with baking parchment. Sprinkle with sliced almonds.

Bake for around 10 minutes.

Chocolate slices

Skurna chokladkakor

AROUND 60 COOKIES

200 G (7 OUNCES) BUTTER OR MARGARINE
2 1/2 DL (1 CUP) SUGAR
5 DL (2 CUPS) ALL-PURPOSE FLOUR
4 TABLESPOONS (1/4 CUP) COCOA
1 TEASPOON BAKING POWDER
1 TABLESPOON VANILLA SUGAR OR
    1 1/2 TEASPOONS VANILLA EXTRACT
1 EGG

Brushing and garnish:
1 EGG, LIGHTLY BEATEN
PEARL SUGAR

Preheat the oven to 200°C (400°F).
Combine all ingredients well. Divide
into six equal parts and form them into
logs. Place on a greased or parchment-
lined baking sheet. Press down to flat-
ten slightly. Brush with beaten egg and
sprinkle with pearl sugar. Bake in the
center of the oven for around 15 minutes. While still warm, cut into 2 cm
(3/4 inch) diagonal lengths.

Currant cookies

Korintkakor

AROUND 90 COOKIES

200 G (7 OUNCES) BUTTER OR MARGARINE
2 DL (1 CUP) SUGAR
2 EGGS
1 1/2 DL (2/3 CUP) CURRANTS, CHOPPED
50 G (2 OUNCES) SEMI-SWEET CHOCOLATE,
    CHOPPED
4 TABLESPOONS (1/4 CUP) CHOPPED
    CANDIED ORANGE PEEL
6 DL (2 1/2 CUPS) ALL-PURPOSE FLOUR
1 TEASPOON BAKING POWDER

Preheat the oven to 175°C (350°F).
Beat butter and sugar until light and
fluffy. Add the eggs, one at a time. Stir
in the currants, chocolate and orange
peel. Combine flour and baking powder
and add, mixing well.

Place teaspoonfuls of dough onto a
greased or parchment-lined baking
sheet. Bake in the center of the oven
for around 12 minutes.

Dreams

Drömmar

ABOUT 60 COOKIES

200 G (7 OZ) UNSALTED BUTTER,
    SOFTENED
1 1/2 DL (2/3 CUP) SUGAR
1 3/4 TEASPOONS VANILLA EXTRACT
1/2 TEASPOON HORNSALT (AMMONIUM
    CARBONATE) OR 1 1/2 TEASPOONS
    BAKING POWDER
5 DL (2 1/4 CUPS) ALL-PURPOSE FLOUR

Preheat the oven to 150°C (300°F).
Line a baking sheet with baking parchment. Beat butter, sugar and vanilla
until light and fluffy. Dissolve hornsalt
in 1 teaspoon water and add. Add flour
and knead until smooth. Divide dough
into three equal parts and make 20
balls from each. Place on parchment
and press each cookie lightly with a wet
finger. Bake about 20 minutes.

Caramel slices

Kolakakor

AROUND 30 COOKIES

100 G (3 1/2 OUNCES) UNSALTED BUTTER
1 DL (1/2 CUP) SUGAR
2 1/2 DL (1 CUP) ALL-PURPOSE FLOUR
1 TABLESPOON DARK CORN SYRUP
1 TEASPOON BAKING SODA

Preheat the oven to 200°C (400°F).
Combine all ingredients well. Divide in
half and roll each piece into lengths on
a floured board. Place on baking parchment and press down lightly. Place them
far enough apart so they don't run
together while baking. Bake for around
10 minutes. Immediately cut into 2 cm
(3/4 inch) lengths. It is also possible to
make separate cookies. Roll the dough
into small balls and place on a parchment-lined baking sheet. Press down
lightly. Bake for around 8 minutes.

To retain the chewy texture of these
cookies, store in an airtight tin. For dry
cookies, leave off the lid!

Lent

There's an old saying that Christmas lasts until Easter. But we know that's not true, because Lent comes in-between. In the past, that meant 40 days with no meat on the table and no fun at all. The prelude to that, just before the start of Lent, was as close as we could ever come to a real latin carnival this far north. This included three days of music, dancing and spectacles – and lots of food! The feasting began on "pork Sunday, continued through "bun Monday" and ended on Shrove Tuesday. Today we celebrate Shrove Tuesday by gorging on buns filled with whipped cream and almond paste. But don't overdo it. In 1771, King Adolf Fredrik, the father of Gustav III, loved those buns so much that he ate himself to death.

CHRISTER LINGSTRÖM:
"Lenten buns and crayfish are two of my favorite foods. I can go all year craving these wonderful buns filled with cream and almond paste. I like to serve them in warm milk with a hint of coffee. Even though many bakeries start selling them right after Christmas, I don't believe in compromising. I wait until Shrove Tuesday!"

Lenten buns

Semlor

AROUND 15 BUNS

100 G (3 1/2 OUNCES) BUTTER
3 DL (1 1/4 CUPS) MILK
50 G (1 3/4 OUNCES) FRESH YEAST
1/2 TEASPOON SALT
1 DL (SCANT 1/2 CUP) SUGAR
1 EGG
1/2 TEASPOON AMMONIUM CARBONATE
   (OR 1 1/2 TEASPOONS BAKING POWDER)
1 LITER (4 1/4 CUPS) ALL-PURPOSE FLOUR

For brushing:
1 EGG, BEATEN

Filling 1:
150 G (5 OUNCES) ALMOND PASTE

Filling 2:
125 G (4 OUNCES) CHOPPED ALMONDS
CRUMBS FROM THE INTERIOR OF THE BUNS
AROUND 1 DL (1/2 CUP) HOT MILK
1 DL (SCANT 1/2 CUP) SUGAR

Garnish:
2 DL (1 CUP) WHIPPING CREAM
POWDERED SUGAR

Melt the butter and add the milk. Heat to 37 °C (98 °F). Crumble the yeast into a large bowl. Add salt, sugar, melted butter, milk and the egg. Combine the ammonium carbonate and flour and knead into the dough. Knead until smooth and elastic, 4–5 minutes. Let rise in the bowl for around 30 minutes.

Preheat the oven to 170 °C (350 °F). Turn the dough onto a floured board and knead a little more for a lighter result. Divide into 15 equal parts and roll into balls. Place on greased baking sheets. Brush with beaten egg. Bake in the center of the oven for 8–10 minutes. Let cool. Cut off the top and scoop out the center of each bun.

Divide the almond paste among the buns. If it is too stiff, beat in a little of the cream. Or mix the chopped almonds with milk and sugar.

Whip the cream. Pipe or spoon whipped cream on top of the almond filling. Replace the top of the bun. Sift powdered sugar over.

Waffle day

This day is probably the fortunate result of a misunderstanding. During the Middle Ages, Annunciation Day was called "Spring Friday", which sounded like" waffle day". They don't sound at all alike in English, but they do in Swedish! And lucky for us, because warm, newly baked waffles with strawberry preserves are hard to beat! Annunciation Day falls on March 25. Since around 400 AD, "Lady Day" (formally, the Annunciation of the Virgin Mary) has been celebrated as the day that the angel Gabriel told Mary that she would bear a son.

CHRISTER LINGSTRÖM:
"Unlike Lenten buns, waffles can be eaten year-round. Served with anchovies and sour cream instead of whipped cream and preserves, they make a great starter. And with a fruit salad, they are a fine dessert. It's important to follow the recipe exactly. Sparkling water or even snow gives the waffles the right texture."

Waffles

Våfflor

AROUND 8 WAFFLES

75 G (3 OUNCES) BUTTER
+ BUTTER FOR THE IRON
2 DL (1 CUP) ICE-COLD SPARKLING WATER
4 DL (2 CUPS) ALL-PURPOSE FLOUR
3 DL (1 1/2 CUPS) WHIPPING CREAM

Melt the butter and let it cool.

Whisk together sparkling water and flour. Stir in the butter.

Lightly whip the cream and fold carefully into the batter.

Heat the waffle iron and brush with butter. Make the waffles. Place the finished waffles on a rack to keep them crispy. Stack right before serving.

Strawberry jam:
4 LITERS (1 GALLON) STRAWBERRIES
12 DL (4 1/2 CUPS) SUGAR
1/2 TEASPOON SODIUM BENZOATE

Clean the berries. Rinse as needed. Layer with the sugar in a large pot. Let rest for a few hours to allow the berries to release their juice. Slowly heat to boiling and let simmer for 15 minutes. Shake and turn the pot to heat the mixture evenly. Skim well. When the jam is finished cooking, the berries should be plump with sugared juice and sink to the bottom.

Dissolve the benzoate in a small amount of the strawberry mixture. Stir into the berries. Pack in hot, clean jars. Seal.

Easter

If you open the door on Maundy Thursday and meet a little girl dressed up as a witch with a coffeepot, you know that it's Easter in Sweden. The real Easter witches weren't quite so charming. During Maundy Thursday night, witches used to pay their taxes in butter to the devil at Brocken mountain. They flew there on broomsticks that were greased with a secret salve. They came and went through the chimney, and in order to disappear like greased lightning, each witch had to recite a magic formula.

Eggs play an important role in the celebration of Easter and are always served on the eve of the holiday. A chick pecking out of its shell was seen as a symbol of life and it appears in food, as decoration, things to paint, candy and as packaging for candy. Salmon, lamb, herring, smoked herring and Jansson's temptation also have a place on the Swedish Easter table. The date of Easter Sunday is determined by the first full moon after the solstice, which means between March 22 and April 25.

CHRISTER LINGSTRÖM:
"Serve a buffet, just as at Christmas, so you have time to be with your guests. Let your imagination be your guide when stuffing eggs. And think yellow when you decorate your Easter cake – a few chickens on top make a great impression."

Fresh eggs on the Easter table

You can color eggs yellow by adding grated carrot and turmeric to the cooking water. For blue-lilac eggs, use blueberries. For brown, use onion skins, and for red, use grated beets in the cooking water.

Cooking eggs

For the best consistency, eggs should simmer, never boil. If eggs are cooked at a rolling boil, the shells will crack easily and the whites will be hard and tough.

Cooking times for eggs starting with cold water:
Soft-cooked eggs take 3–5 minutes, hard-cooked 7–8 minutes from the time the water begins to boil.

Different degrees of soft-cooked eggs:
Three minutes: About half the egg white will be cooked, while the remaining white and the yolk will be runny. Five minutes: The entire white will be cooked, while the yolk will be creamy.

Hard-cooked eggs:
Both the whites and the yolks will be solid and cooked through.
Hard-cooked eggs should not be stored for more than 2–3 days in the refrigerator.

A test for freshness:
Place the egg in water. A fresh egg lies on the bottom. A week-old egg floats halfway up the water, while a three-week-old egg sits in the water with the blunt end up. If the egg floats right to the top, it is old and should not be eaten.

Storage:
Eggs absorb aromas from other foods very easily and should not be stored with strong-smelling foodstuffs such as onions and smoked sausages. However, placing eggs in a jar with fresh truffles creates an unbelievable flavor sensation!

Stuffed eggs

These can be varied endlessly. Here are six suggestions, clockwise from the top:

Top with a rolled anchovy or fillet and finely chopped chives.

Top with a spoonful of whitefish caviar. Garnish with dill and chopped red onion.

Top with cold-smoked salmon, lemon and grated horseradish.

Mash the yolk and mix with finely chopped chives, whitefish caviar and a dollop of whipped cream.

Top with shrimp, a dollop of mayonnaise and dill.

Top with marinated herring, onion and dill.

Classic marinated herring

Klassisk inlagd sill

2 SALT HERRING FILLETS (OR PRESOAKED
   HERRING FILLETS, FROM A JAR
   OR DEFROSTED)
1 RED ONION
1 CARROT
CHUNK HORSERADISH
15 ALLSPICE BERRIES
10 WHITE PEPPERCORNS
2 BAY LEAVES
8–12 WHOLE CLOVES

Brine:
1 1/2 DL (3/4 CUP) WATER
1 DL (1/2 CUP) VINEGAR ESSENCE (12%)
1 1/2 DL (3/4 CUP) SUGAR

Soak the salt herring fillets in cold water for 24 hours, changing the water at least twice. (Or use presoaked fillets.)

Combine water, vinegar essence and sugar. If vinegar essence is not available, use 2 1/2 dl (1 cup) plain pickling vinegar. Heat to boiling and let cool.

Rinse the herring. Drain. Cut into 2–3 cm (1 inch) wide slices. Cut the onion and carrot into thin slices. Cut the horseradish into small dice.

Layer herring, carrot, horseradish and seasonings in a jar. Pour over the cold brine and seal.

Refrigerate for 24–48 hours. Serve with aged cheese and boiled potatoes.

In the picture, the brine has been colored with beet juice.

Smoked salmon with scrambled eggs and chives

Rökt lax med äggröra smaksatt med gräslök

4 SERVINGS (AS A STARTER)

4 EGGS
1 TABLESPOON BUTTER
1/2 DL (3 1/2 TABLESPOONS) WHIPPING
   CREAM
SALT AND PEPPER
2–3 TABLESPOONS FINELY CHOPPED
   CHIVES
AROUND 350 G (12 OUNCES)
   COLD-SMOKED SALMON
1/2 RED ONION, CHOPPED
2 TABLESPOONS CAPERS
DILL

Beat the eggs. Melt the butter. Add the eggs and stir slowly until creamy and almost cooked through. Stir in the cream, salt, pepper and chives.

Arrange the salmon on individual plates. Top with scrambled eggs. Garnish with chopped red onion, capers and dill. Serve with toast.

Roast lamb

Lammstek

8 SERVINGS

2 KG (4 1/2 POUNDS) BONED LEG OF LAMB
1 DL (1/2 CUP) CHOPPED FRESH PARSLEY
3/4 DL (1/3 CUP) CHOPPED FRESH THYME
2 TABLESPOONS FRESH ROSEMARY
10 GARLIC CLOVES, SLICED
2 TABLESPOONS BUTTER
1 1/2 TEASPOONS SALT
1/2 TEASPOON PEPPER

Preheat the oven to 180°C (350°F).
Trim the meat. Combine parsley,
thyme, rosemary and garlic. Sprinkle
over the meat. Roll up and tie. Brown
on all sides in butter. Season with salt
and pepper. Roast for 30–40 minutes.

Skim fat from the pan juices and serve
with the meat.

Hasselback potatoes

Hasselbackspotatis

4 SERVINGS

8–12 OVAL POTATOES
3 TABLESPOONS BUTTER OR MARGARINE
1–1 1/2 TEASPOONS SALT
1 TABLESPOON BREADCRUMBS
2 TABLESPOONS GRATED HARD CHEESE

Preheat the oven to 225°C (425°F).
Peel and rinse the potatoes. Cut each
into thin slices almost all the way
through – the potato should stay
together at the base. This is simplest
if you place the potato in a wooden
spoon or against a thin cutting board
to stop the knife from cutting all the
way through.

Melt the butter in an ovenproof dish.
Arrange the potatoes with the cut
side up. Brush with melted butter and
sprinkle with salt. Bake for 30 minutes.
Combine breadcrumbs and grated
cheese and sprinkle over the potatoes.
Bake for 10–15 minutes more.

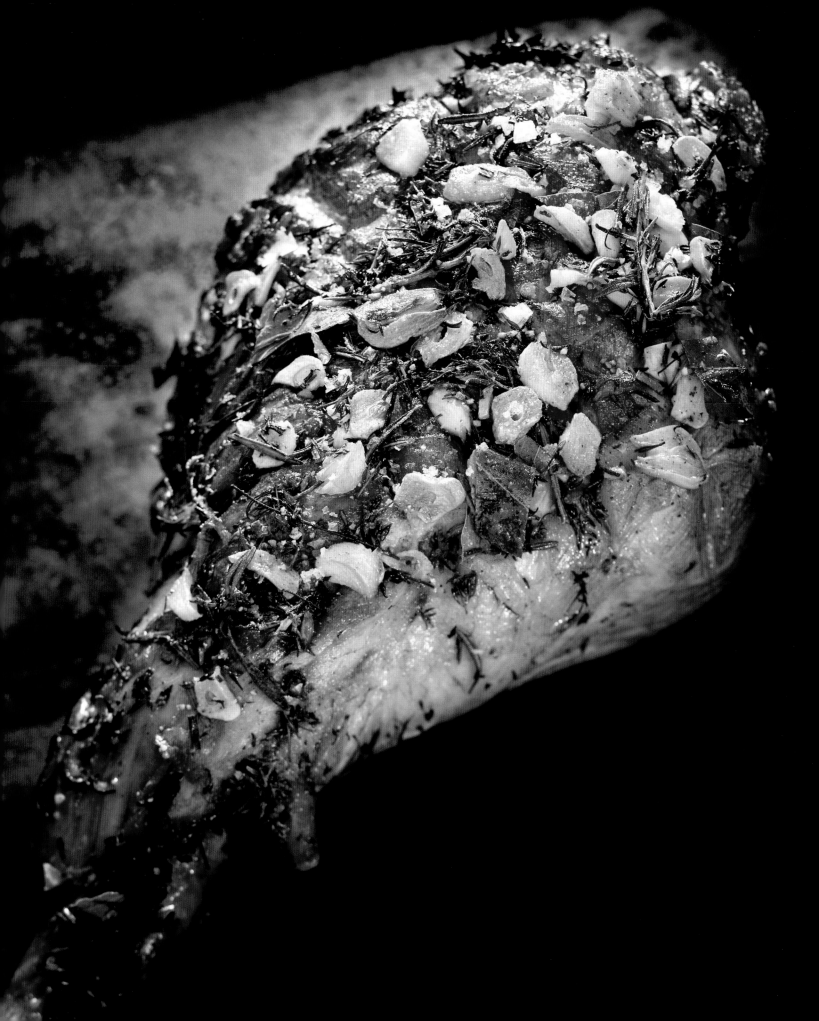

Easter cake

Påsktårta

Cake base:
3 EGGS
3 DL (1 1/4 CUPS) SUGAR
3 DL (1 1/4 CUPS) ALL-PURPOSE FLOUR
2 TEASPOONS BAKING POWDER
7 TABLESPOONS BOILING WATER

Preheat the oven to 175°C (350°F).
Grease and flour a 24–26 cm (9–10
inch) springform pan. Beat eggs and
sugar until light and lemon-colored.
Combine flour and baking powder and
add, mixing lightly. Add the boiling
water, mixing until combined. Pour into
the prepared pan. Bake for around 25
minutes. Let cool. When completely
cool, cut horizontally into three layers.
Use a long knife and cut carefully all
around and then toward the center.

Filling:
50 G (3 1/2 TABLESPOONS) SOFT BUTTER
50 G (1 3/4 OUNCES) ALMOND PASTE
5 TABLESPOONS (1/3 CUP) POWDERED
    SUGAR
3 TABLESPOONS GRAND MARNIER OR
    OTHER ORNAGE-FLAVORED LIQUEUR
JUICE OF 1/2 ORANGE
2 TABLESPOONS GOOD QUALITY COCOA
    POWDER

Beat butter, almond paste and powdered sugar until light and fluffy. Add
the remaining ingredients, beating until
smooth. Spread half the filling over the
bottom layer. Top with the middle layer
and spread with the remaining filling.
Top with the top layer, pressing down
lightly. Refrigerate.

Frosting:
2 DL (3/4 CUP) WHIPPING CREAM
200 G (7 OUNCES) SEMI-SWEET
    CHOCOLATE
JUICE OF 1/2 ORANGE

Melt all ingredients together over low
heat, stirring often. Spread over the
cold cake.

Garnish:
MARZIPAN CHICKENS
MARZIPAN EGGS
EDIBLE FLOWERS, IF AVAILABLE

Garnish with the above and refrigerate
until serving.

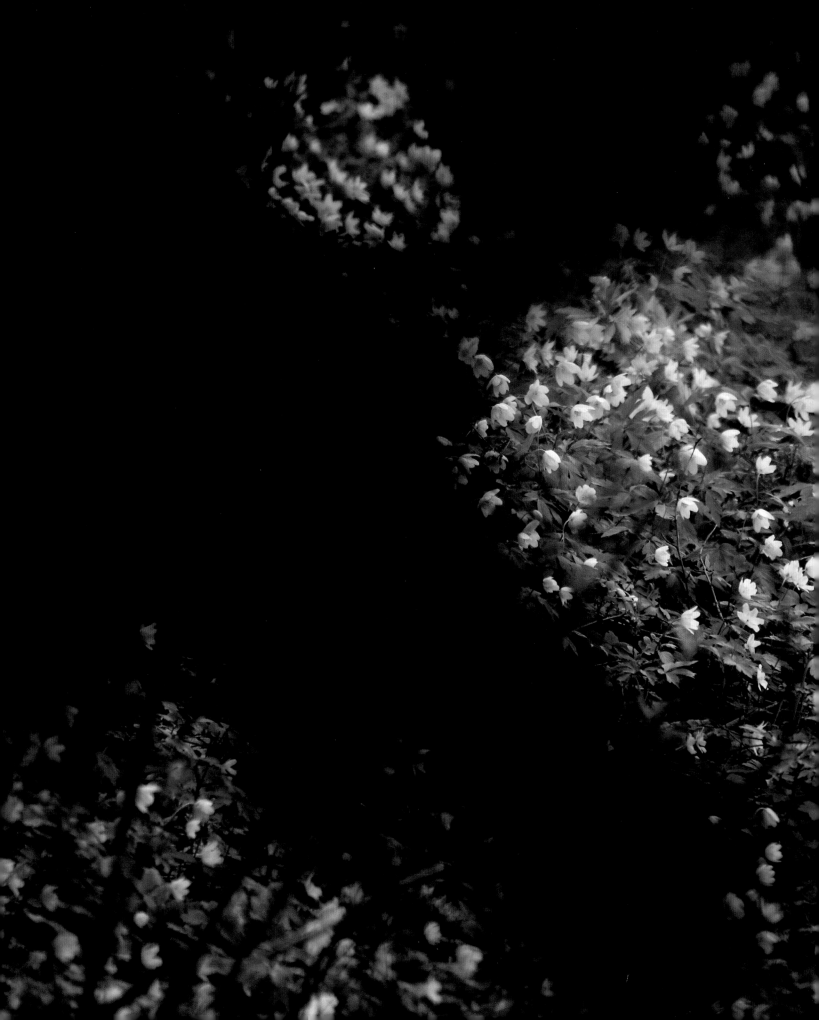

Walpurgis eve (the eve of May Day)

There is no time of year as welcome as the Swedish spring. It doesn't matter if it rains, snows or hails. When the bonfire is lit on Walpurgis eve and the chorus starts to sing, summer can begin. In the olden days, cows were let out to pasture that very evening, and people lit bonfires to scare away wild animals, witches and trolls. What used to be scaring tactics are now the May Day bonfires that all generations of Swedes gather around on the last night of April. The day honors Saint Walpurga (Valborg in Swedish), an English princess who became an abbess in Germany during the 700s and was declared a saint after her death. It is also King Carl Gustav's birthday!

CHRISTER LINGSTRÖM:
"There's no holiday that sparks the culinary imagination like Valborg. Morel soup, spring chicken, nettles, salmon, rhubarb with custard. The variations are endless. For me personally, this evening has a special meaning. Exactly 25 years ago, in 1983, I stood on the steps of Edsbacka Krog and welcomed the first guests."

Nettle soup with poached eggs

Nässelsoppa med pocherat ägg

4 SERVINGS

2 LITERS (8 CUPS) TINY NETTLE LEAVES
I 1/2 LITERS (6 CUPS) CHICKEN STOCK
2 SHALLOTS
2 TABLESPOONS BUTTER
I TEASPOON GROUND ANISE
I TEASPOON GROUND FENNEL
I/2 DL (I/4 CUP) CHOPPED CHIVES
SALT AND PEPPER (OPTIONAL)

Clean and rinse the nettles well. Heat the stock to boiling. Coarsely chop the shallots. Sauté nettles and shallots in a little of the butter in a soup pot. Add the stock, anise and fennel. Let boil for a few minutes. Using an immersion blender, mix with chives and the remaining butter until pureed. Season with salt and pepper. Serve with poached eggs.

Poached eggs:
I–I 1/2 LITERS (4–6 CUPS) WATER
I/2 TEASPOON SALT
I TEASPOON VINEGAR
4 EGGS

Combine water, salt and vinegar and heat to boiling. Reduce heat slightly. Crack each egg into a small cup, then gently ease it into the simmering water, guiding the white over to enclose the yolk. Simmer for 3 minutes. Transfer the poached eggs to cold water.

Baked salmon with the flavor of springtime

Ugnsbakad lax med smak
av försommaren

4 SERVINGS

600 G (1 1/3 POUNDS) SKINLESS
    AND BONELESS SALMON FILLET
OIL
COARSE SALT

Preheat the oven to 175 °C (350 °F).
Divide the salmon into four pieces of
equal size and place in a greased ovenproof dish. Sprinkle with salt and bake
for around 10 minutes.

Morel sauce:
50 G (1 3/4 OUNCES) DRIED MORELS
1 SHALLOT
BUTTER
2 DL (3/4 CUP) FISH STOCK
3 DL (1 1/4 CUPS) WHIPPING CREAM
SALT AND PEPPER, CAYENNE PEPPER
    (OPTIONAL)

Pour boiling water over the morels and
let soak for 30 minutes. Drain. Rinse
well to remove any sand. Heat water to
boiling. Add the morels and blanch for
5 minutes. Drain and discard cooking
water. Chop. Chop the shallot and sauté
in a little butter until shiny but not
brown. Add the morels and sauté for
a few minutes. Add stock and cream
and reduce until slightly thickened.
Season with salt, pepper and cayenne
pepper, if desired.

Asparagus:
16 STALKS

Cut off the white tough parts of the
asparagus stalk and peel the lower half.
Cook in lightly salted water for 4–5
minutes.

New potatoes:
Rinse and peel the potatoes and place
in boiling salted water. Return to
boiling, lower heat and let simmer for
around 25 minutes.

Drain. Place a paper towel over the
potatoes and cover with a lid. Let the
potatoes steam for a few minutes. Serve
immediately.

Rhubarb crumble

Smulpaj med rabarber

6 SERVINGS

2 DL (1 CUP) ALL-PURPOSE FLOUR
2 TABLESPOONS SUGAR
100 G (3 1/2 OUNCES) BUTTER
3–4 RHUBARB STALKS, DICED
1 1/2 DL (2/3 CUP) SUGAR
1 TABLESPOON POTATO STARCH
  (OR CORNSTARCH)

Preheat the oven to 220 °C (425 °F).
Combine flour and sugar. Cut in the
butter, mixing until coarse crumbs.

Combine rhubarb, sugar and potato
starch and place in an ovenproof dish.
Sprinkle with the crumb mixture. Bake
for 20–25 minutes.

Serve with vanilla sauce.

Vanilla sauce

Vaniljsås

4 SERVINGS

1 VANILLA BEAN
2 1/2 DL (1 CUP) LIGHT CREAM
4–5 TABLESPOONS SUGAR
3 EGG YOLKS

Split the vanilla bean lengthwise and
scrape out the seeds. Place seeds and
bean in a saucepan with the cream and
heat to boiling.

Whisk sugar and egg yolks together in
a separate saucepan.

Whisk in the vanilla milk and heat to
simmering, stirring constantly. Do not
allow to boil after the egg yolks have
been added. Strain and refrigerate until
serving.

Whitsuntide

Whitsuntide or Pentecost comes on the 50th day after Easter. The word Pentecost comes from the Greek word for 50. This is a popular weekend for weddings, but now – between the flowering of the bird-cherry and the lilac – even nature is a bride. This is a great time for grilling and for picnics, when we can sit outside and enjoy the light, beautiful Nordic nights once again.

CHRISTER LINGSTRÖM:
"Salmon is at its best, nettles are blooming, morels are growing and nature's food basket has so much to offer. All the same, I like to serve the most Swedish dish of all, Toast Skagen. It was invented by chance in 1956 during a boat race when the grand old man of Swedish gastronomy, Tore Wretman, had to compose a lunch with the few ingredients he found in the galley: shrimp, whitefish caviar, mayonnaise and dill."

Toast Skagen

Toast Skagen

4 SERVINGS

This classic and very Scandinavian
toast appeared on a resturant meny
for the first time at Riche in Stockholm
in 1958.

The shrimp should be large and newly
shelled, the mayonnaise fresh and
the slices of bread lightly crunchy.
Although this starter can wait a short
time for guests, it should not dry out
and look tired. It should be fresh as
a sea breeze. And with the caviar as
a crown!

AROUND 400 G (14 OUNCES) FRESH LARGE
   SHRIMP
2 DL (1 CUP) MAYONNAISE
SALT AND FRESHLY GROUND WHITE PEPPER
1 LEMON, CUT INTO 4 THIN WEDGES,
   THE REST JUICED
2 TABLESPOONS FINELY CHOPPED DILL
   PLUS DILL SPRIGS FOR GARNISH
4 SLICES WHITE BREAD
BUTTER
4 TABLESPOONS WHITEFISH OR GOLDEN
   CAVIAR, AROUND 60 G (2 OUNCES)

Shell the shrimp. If they are very large,
chop coarsely and combine with the
mayonnaise. Season with salt, pepper
and lemon juice, and fold in the dill.
Cover and refrigerate until serving
time.

Remove the bread crusts or cut four
circles of bread with a large drinking
glass. Fry in butter until crunchy and
brown.

Place the toast on individual plates.
Top with the shrimp mixture. Garnish
with caviar, lemon wedges and dill
sprigs.

Poached salmon

Inkokt lax

4 SERVINGS

1 SALMON FILLET FROM THE CENTER,
   500 G (1 1/4 POUNDS) AS A STARTER,
   800 G (1 3/4 POUNDS) AS A MAIN COURSE

Brine:
1 MEDIUM CARROT
1 ONION
2 1/2 LITERS (10 CUPS) WATER
1/2 DL (1/4 CUP) RED WINE VINEGAR
1 TABLESPOON SALT
5 WHITE PEPPERCORNS
6 WHOLE CLOVES
1 BAY LEAF
8 DILL STALKS

Remoulade sauce:
1 RAW EGG YOLK
1 HARD-COOKED EGG, FINELY CHOPPED
1 TABLESPOON SWEET SWEDISH MUSTARD
2 DL (3/4 CUP) OIL
1 TEASPOON SUGAR
2 TABLESPOONS WHITE WINE VINEGAR
SALT AND PEPPER
2 TABLESPOONS WHIPPED CREAM
2 TABLESPOONS FINELY CHOPPED DILL

Garnish:
1 GELATIN SHEET
1 DL (1/2 CUP) FISH STOCK
DILL

Peel the carrot and cut into coins. Peel the onion and cut into wedges. Combine all ingredients for the brine and boil for 10 minutes. Cut the salmon into four pieces of equal size and place in a pan. Add brine to cover the salmon completely. Reheat to boiling, then remove from the heat. Cover and let the salmon cool in the brine. Refrigerate, leaving the salmon to continue marinating for several hours.

For the sauce: All ingredients should be the same temperature. Place the egg yolk, the egg and the mustard in a bowl. Gradually beat in the oil, a little at a time. Add the sugar and vinegar and season with salt and pepper. Fold in the whipped cream and dill. Refrigerate for one hour before serving.

Remove the salmon from the brine and drain. Garnish with cooked carrots and leeks. Soak the gelatin in cold water for around 5 minutes. Heat the fish stock and add the gelatin, stirring until melted. Remove from the heat and let cool until it begins to solidify. Brush the salmon with the gelatin mixture. Refrigerate until stiff.

Check the sauce for seasoning, as the acidity can lessen while it is in the refrigerator. Serve with remoulade sauce and garnish with dill. For extra color, chop a few carrot coins from the brine and sprinkle over the remoulade sauce. New potatoes and pickles are good with this dish.

Roast chicken
with cream sauce

Stekt vårkyckling med gräddsås

4 SERVINGS

I CHICKEN, AROUND I.2 KG (2 I/2 POUNDS)
A FEW PARSLEY STALKS
SALT AND PEPPER
I TABLESPOON BUTTER

Sauce:
CHICKEN BONES
I/2 TABLESPOON BUTTER
I TEASPOON ALL-PURPOSE FLOUR
I I/2 DL (3/4 CUP) CHICKEN STOCK
2 DL (I CUP) WHIPPING CREAM

Side dishes:
FRIED POTATOES
CURRANT JELLY
CUCUMBER SALAD

Preheat the oven to 185°C (375°F).
Stuff the chicken with parsley, salt
and pepper

Brown the chicken in butter and transfer to the oven. Roast on one side first,
then on the other and finally with the
breast up. The chicken is cooked when
the juices run clear with no trace of
pink. This takes around 40 minutes for
a chicken of this size. Carve the chick-
en into two legs and two breasts.

Cut the carcass into pieces. Melt the
butter in a pot. Add the carcass, sprinkle with flour and stir over low heat.
Add the stock and let simmer for 5
minutes, stirring often. Add the cream
and simmer for 5 minutes more.

Transfer the chicken pieces to a platter.
Strain the sauce. Season to taste and
serve with fried potatoes, jelly and
marinated cucumber salad (see recipe
on page 60).

42

Vanilla ice cream

Vaniljglass

20 SERVINGS

2 VANILLA BEANS
1 LITER (QUART) HALF AND HALF
3 TABLESPOONS HONEY
1 GELATIN SHEET
10 EGG YOLKS
2 1/2 DL (1 CUP) SUGAR

Split the vanilla beans lengthwise and scrape out the seeds. Place seeds and beans in a saucepan with the half and half and honey and heat to boiling. Soften the gelatin in cold water.

Beat egg yolks and sugar until light and lemon-colored. Whisk the hot half and half into the egg mixture. Pour into a clean saucepan and heat, whisking constantly, until it reaches around 80°C (175°F), or until the mixture is slightly thickened and coats the back of a wooden spoon. Add the gelatin, stirring until melted. Refrigerate for around 6 hours. Strain. Freeze in an ice cream machine.

Sweden's national day

In 2004, the Swedish Parliament passed a law establishing Sweden's national day, June 6, as a holiday. For a national day, it was very young, only 22 years old, but it had been celebrated as "Swedish Flag Day" since 1916. The first celebration took place in the presence of King Gustav V at Stockholm stadium, where the Olympic Games had been arranged four years earlier. In 1963, Skansen took over as the site for the celebration, and the royal family still participate in the yearly festivities. On June 6, 1523, Gustav Vasa was proclaimed king of Sweden, and on that day in 1809, the constitution was written.

CHRISTER LINGSTRÖM:
"This is the perfect opportunity to serve something Swedish, or why not visit a small town in our long and narrow country and dine at a hotel or inn and eat something unquestionably Swedish, such as marinated salmon with mustard sauce followed by meatballs with cream sauce, lingonberries and pickles."

Meatballs

Köttbullar

4–6 SERVINGS

1 DL (1/2 CUP) SOFT BREADCRUMBS
  (FROM DAY-OLD BREAD)
2 DL (1 CUP) MILK
200 G (8 OUNCES) LEAN GROUND BEEF
100 G (4 OUNCES) GROUND VEAL
100 G (4 OUNCES) GROUND PORK
SALT AND WHITE PEPPER
1/2 ONION, MINCED
BUTTER AND OIL FOR FRYING
1 EGG

Soak the breadcrumbs in the milk. Add the ground meat, 1 teaspoon salt and 1/4 teaspoon ground pepper.

Brown the onion in a little butter. Let cool and stir into the meat mixture.

Add the egg, stirring to mix. Add a little water, if necessary.

Make a trial meatball. Fry in browned butter and taste. Adjust seasoning if necessary. If the ball is too hard, add a little water and try again. Don't give up until you are completely satisfied.

Roll the mixture into relatively large balls, around 30 g (1 ounce) each, if you are serving them as a main course. Make them smaller for a buffet or Christmas table. As you form them, place the meatballs on a rinsed cutting board, so they won't stick.

Heat a frying pan and add oil, then butter. Brown the meatballs, shaking the pan often, so they roll around and brown equally on all sides.

Accompaniments are a matter of taste. Mashed potatoes, brown beans, brown gravy or cream sauce with lingonberries and pickles. They are all delicious with meatballs.

Some advice:
Let the ground meat mixture rest. Make it several hours before frying so it can rest and the tastes can meld.

Be careful with onion. Raw onion ferments in ground meat, so be sure to brown the onion if you plan to freeze the meatballs. If you plan to eat the meatballs the same day they're made, then you can use raw onion.

Butter and oil are best for pan-frying. When I fry meatballs, I used a mixture of butter and oil. I can then increase the frying temperature and the meatballs brown more evenly, they develop a better color, and they are juicier and tastier.

The Swedish Dala horse

The first time the Dala horse was mentioned abroad was as Sweden's contribution to the 1939 World's Fair in New York. Back then, it was 3 meters high. Today there are small Dala horses in homes from Sydney to Dar-es-Salaam, brought back by their owners after a trip to Sweden or received as a gift from Swedish guests.

This famous wooden horse first appeared during the 1700s as a sideline of the cabinetmakers in Dalarna.

Its characteristic appearance was influenced by the richly decorated painted floral motifs popular at that time. The traditional pattern, the so-called ripple, is still painted by hand. If you want to watch these horses being made, you should visit Nusnäs, 10 kilometers south of Mora in Dalarna.

Midsummer

The most relaxed of all Swedish holidays is Midsummer. That's the longest day of the year, and sun never sets in the north. According to folklore, elves dance in the fields on Midsummer night and nature is filled with trolldom and has healing powers. The maypole (or more correctly in Swedish, "the midsummer pole") is at the center of the festivities. It is decorated in the morning and set up later in the day. People jumping around a leafy pole like small frogs can be seen only in Sweden, in Åland, in Swedish-speaking areas of Finland – and in cities in Bavaria. The maypole came to Sweden from Germany in the 1600s and is today, along with Lucia and the Dala horse, the most Swedish of all our national symbols.

CHRISTER LINGSTRÖM:
"On Midsummer evenings, I am always in Dalarna, at the heart of Swedish midsummer celebrations. Every summer a group of chefs and colleagues get together on this night, so there is a lot of food. Matjes herring, new potatoes and strawberries are the mainstays of the buffet. Plus everything else that's in season. Midsummer is the best time of year to test the new schnapps with our beer. The best ones are those we have spiced ourselves."

Matjes herring for the buffet

Matjessill för buffébordet

3–4 MATJES HERRING FILLETS

Sauce:
1 DL (1/2 CUP) WHIPPING CREAM
1 DL (1/2 CUP) SOUR CREAM
1 TABLESPOON MUSTARD
1 TABLESPOON CAPERS
1 SMALL ONION, CHOPPED
2 HARD-COOKED EGGS, CHOPPED
1/4 TEASPOON SALT AND WHITE PEPPER
DILL SPRIGS

Drain the herring and cut into 2–3 cm (1 inch) diagonal slices. Whip the cream and stir in the sour cream. Add mustard, capers, onion and egg, mixing well. Season with salt and pepper.

Arrange the herring on a plate. Pour over the sauce and garnish with fresh dill.

Served with boiled new potatoes, whole grain rye bread, butter and cheese.

Matjes herring with pickles

Matjessill med pickles

3–4 SERVINGS

3–4 MATJES HERRING FILLETS
AROUND 1 DL (1/2 CUP) PICKLES
1 DL (1/2 CUP) MAYONNAISE
2 TABLESPOONS SOUR CREAM
1 TABLESPOON FINELY CHOPPED DILL

Drain the herring and cut into slices. Coarsely chop the pickles. Combine with the remaining ingredients.

Serve at a buffet with other dishes.

Matjes herring in the traditional way

Matjessill på traditionellt sätt

2–4 SERVINGS

200 G (8 OUNCES) MATJES HERRING
　FILLETS
2 HARD-COOKED EGGS, COLD
1 DL (1/2 CUP) SOUR CREAM
CHIVES

Drain the herring, cut into pieces and
place on a dish.

Peel and chop the eggs.

Arrange the eggs, sour cream and
chives on the dish alongside the herring

Serve new potatoes cooked with dill
with this dish.

Warm matjes herring

Varm matjessill

4 SERVINGS

3–4 MATJES HERRING FILLETS
2 RED ONIONS
2 HARD-COOKED EGGS
4 BOILED POTATOES
DILL SPRIGS
FINELY CHOPPED CHIVES
MELTED BUTTER

Drain the herring and cut into pieces.
Slice the onions, eggs and potatoes.
Arrange all ingredients on a plate.
Just before serving, drizzle with melted
butter.

Summer matjes herring

Sommarmatjessill

4 SERVINGS

3–4 MATJES HERRING FILLETS
1 APPLE
1 PICKLE
1 TOMATO
1 1/2 DL (2/3 CUP) MAYONNAISE
1–2 TEASPOONS GRATED HORSERADISH

Drain the herring and arrange them
whole or in pieces on a plate. Peel
and chop the apple, pickle and tomato
and combine.

Thin the mayonnaise with 2–3 tablespoons water and stir into the apple,
pickle and tomato. Season with horseradish.

Just before serving, pour over the
herring. Serve at a buffet with other
dishes.

Sauce for smoked salmon or smoked char

Sås till rökt lax
eller rökt röding

4 SERVINGS

2 DL (1 CUP) SOUR CREAM
   OR CRÈME FRAICHE
1/2 DL (1/4 CUP) MAYONNAISE
3 TABLESPOONS FINELY CHOPPED CHIVES
   OR DILL
2 TABLESPOONS DIJON MUSTARD
WHITEFISH CAVIAR
SALT AND PEPPER

Combine all ingredients.

Serve with smoked fish along with
boiled potatoes and cucumber salad.

Cucumber salad:
1 SEEDLESS CUCUMBER
1 TABLESPOON SALT
2 1/2 DL (1 CUP) VINEGAR
1 1/4 DL (1/2 CUP) SUGAR
1 DL (1/2 CUP) MINCED PARSLEY

Peel vertical strips off the cucumber all
around so that it looks striped when
cut. Slice thinly with a cheese plane.
Sprinkle with salt and place between
two flat dishes for 1 hour. Drain. Mix
vinegar and sugar together and add the
cucumber and parsley.

Strawberry torte

Jordgubbstårta

10–12 SERVINGS

SPONGE BASE, SEE RECIPE ON PAGE 26

Filling:
250 G (9 OUNCES) QUARK OR CREAMED
   COTTAGE CHEESE, SIEVED
SEEDS FROM 1 VANILLA BEAN
1 DL (1/2 CUP) STRAWBERRY PRESERVES
GRATED ZEST FROM 2 ORANGES
1 SPONGE BASE, DIVIDED HORIZONTALLY
   INTO TWO LAYERS
CONCENTRATED STRAWBERRY JUICE
5 DL (2 CUPS) WHIPPING CREAM
AROUND 1 KG (2 1/4 POUNDS) FRESH
   STRAWBERRIES, SLICED

Combine quark, vanilla seeds, preserves and orange zest. Place the lower half of the sponge base, cut side up, on a platter. Drizzle with a little concentrated strawberry juice. Spread with the filling. Drizzle concentrated strawberry juice over the cut side of the remaining cake half and place, cut side down, on the filling.

Whip the cream. Spread over the entire cake. Garnish with sliced strawberries and refrigerate until serving time. Serve with a cup of coffee and a little glass of liqueur.

Crayfish party

Since the 1500s, platters have groaned, dill crowns have swayed and glasses of schnapps have been emptied whenever Swedes have eaten freshwater crayfish in August. There used to be so many crayfish in our waters that we could pluck them by hand. But they didn't become a reason to celebrate until the 1800s, when they became so popular that they needed protection to insure future supplies, and August 8 was declared the first day of the crayfish season! Today we can have crayfish parties year-round, but because a parasitic mold decimated Sweden's crayfish population, most of the 4000 tons of crayfish Swedes consume every year are imported from China, Turkey and Spain.

CHRISTER LINGSTRÖM:
"A real crayfish party should be held under a clear August sky with a full moon, party hats, schnapps and songs. I am absolutely crazy about crayfish and can go around all summer thinking about them and planning parties. Nothing is simpler. After the crayfish have been cooked, you can spend all your time with your guests. Some good advice: Cook the crayfish ahead of time and leave them in the brine for 48 hours instead of eating them newly cooked. The crayfish absorb the aroma of the dill and the salt and develop a fantastic flavor."

Prästost cakes

Prästostkakor

The name of the hard, cow's milk cheese in these cookies translates as "priest cheese". From the 16th to the 19th century, the church made cheese from some of the milk it received as tithes, thus the name.

4 SERVINGS

150 G (5 OUNCES) GRATED PRÄSTOST
    OR OTHER FULL-FLAVORED HARD
    CHEESE, SUCH AS WHITE CHEDDAR
2 EGG YOLKS
2 TABLESPOONS WHIPPING CREAM
SALT AND PEPPER

Combine cheese, egg yolks and cream and season with salt and pepper. It's a good idea to make the batter a day ahead of time and refrigerate overnight.

Preheat the oven to 175 °C (350 °F). Spoon the mixture into four individual ovenproof dishes or into paper baking cups and bake for 5–10 minutes.

Fermented Baltic herring

Fermented Baltic herring smells pungent and rotten. And it is still loved by so many Swedes that demand exceeds supply every year. Surströmming, literally translated as "sour herring", ferment in tins and have a well-rounded spicy flavor. The tins can also be called well-rounded, as they sometimes become almost as round as balls due to all the fermentation inside. The first herring party of the year is always on the third Thursday in August. Classic accompaniments are flatbread, onions, almond potatoes and beer. True enthusiasts are said to prefer milk. For good reason, tins of fermented herring are best opened outdoors!

CHRISTER LINGSTRÖM:
"I remember how my childhood home smelled after my parents' surströmming parties during the 1960s. That's probably why I don't serve it to my friends from abroad. I often make the excuse that I am not grown-up enough to learn to eat it. But don't hesitate if you want to try a genuine Swedish delicacy."

For a "surströmming" party:
SURSTRÖMMING
BOILED ALMOND POTATOES
CHOPPED RED ONION
SOUR CREAM (OPTIONAL)
FLATBREAD, HARD AND SOFT
BUTTER
WHEY CHEESE (CARAMELIZED GOAT CHEESE,
    SUCH AS SKI QUEEN) AND HARD CHEESE

CLOUDBERRY-FILLED ALMOND CAKE
    OR CLOUDBERRIES AND CREAM

BEER AND/OR WATER

You can also eat the herring in a sandwich roll. Layer sliced boiled potatoes, herring and chopped onion on soft flatbread. Roll up and eat like a "wrap".

Cinnamon Roll Day

If we Swedes are so crazy that we dedicate a day of the year to a pastry, there is only one kind of pastry we can be talking about! On Cinnamon Roll Day, October 4, buns rise in homes, at schools, day care centers and everywhere else all over Sweden. The day was established by the Institute for Home Baking in 1999. The object of this adoration, the cinnamon roll, has been a mainstay of many children's party since the 1920s.

CHRISTER LINGSTRÖM:
"A kitchen that smells of cinnamon rolls is a trip back to childhood. But even adults can't resist a cinnamon roll straight from the oven with a cup of freshly brewed coffee."

Cardamom rolls

Kardemummabullar

AROUND 45 ROLLS

Basic dough:
150 G (5 OUNCES) MARGARINE OR BUTTER
5 DL (2 CUPS) MILK
50 G (1 3/4 OUNCES) FRESH YEAST
1/2 TEASPOON SALT
1–1 1/2 DL (1/2–2/3 CUP) SUGAR
2 TEASPOONS GROUND CARDAMOM
AROUND 1.3 LITERS (5 1/2 CUPS)
    ALL-PURPOSE FLOUR

Filling:
1 1/2 TEASPOONS CARDAMOM SEEDS
100–125 G (4 OUNCES) ALMOND PASTE
50 G (3 TABLESPOONS) BUTTER
    OR MARGARINE

Brushing and garnish:
1 EGG
PEARL SUGAR OR CRUSHED SUGAR CUBES

Melt the margarine or butter in a saucepan. Add the milk and heat to lukewarm, around 37 °C (98 °F).

Crumble the yeast into a baking bowl with some of the milk mixture. Add the remaining liquid, salt, sugar, cardamom and around 2/3 of the flour, mixing well.

Knead the dough until it is smooth and elastic. Knead in the remaining flour, but save around 1/2 cup for later. The dough is ready when it pulls away from the sides of the bowl. Sprinkle a little flour over the top so it doesn't dry out. Cover with a cloth and place in a warm, draft-free place and let rise until double.

Knead the dough in the bowl for a few minutes. Turn out onto a floured board. Knead in the remaining flour. The dough is ready when it pulls away from the board and hands. If you slash the dough, the pores should be even. If there are large pores, the dough hasn't been kneaded enough.

Crush the cardamom seeds. Grate the almond paste. Combine for the filling.

Divide the dough in half. Roll each half into a rectangle on a lightly floured board. Spread the filling over the dough. Roll up and cut into even slices. Place them, cut side up, in paper baking cups or on baking parchment. Cover and let rise until double.

Brush with beaten egg and sprinkle with pearl sugar.

Preheat the oven to 250 °C (425 °F). Bake in the center of the oven for 8–10 minutes.

Cinnamon snails

Kanelsnurror

1 BATCH BASIC DOUGH
    (SEE CARDAMOM ROLLS)

Filling:
75–100 G (3 OUNCES) MARGARINE
1 DL (1/3–1/2 CUP) SUGAR
2 TEASPOONS CINNAMON

Brushing and garnish:
1 EGG
PEARL SUGAR OR CRUSHED SUGAR CUBES
CHOPPED ALMONDS

Prepare the basic dough for cardamom rolls.

Combine the ingredients for the filling.

Divide the dough in half. Roll each half into a rectangle on a lightly floured board. Spread the filling over the dough. Roll up and cut into even slices. Place them, cut side up, in paper baking cups or on baking parchment. Cover and let rise until double.

Brush with beaten egg and sprinkle with pearl sugar and almonds. Preheat the oven to 250 °C (425 °F). Bake in the center of the oven for 8–10 minutes.

Martin Goose

Around November 10, Swedish geese are at their plumpest. This holiday is celebrated primarily in southern Sweden, in Skåne. What many don't realize is that Skåne's very own dish was served first in Stockholm. Even Queen Kristina had a Martin Goose party at the Royal Palace in Stockholm.

Before he became a goose, Martin was a French saint. His day was celebrated first in Germany, and eventually the holiday spread to Sweden during the 1500s.

CHRISTER LINGSTRÖM:
"An authentic goose dinner begins with black soup, a spicy sweet and sour soup made from goose or pork blood. I have stirred so many pots of black soup that I have a shoulder injury! As a main course, I serve roast goose with apples and prunes, and for dessert, apple cake from Skåne."

Roast Goose

Gås

8 SERVINGS

1 YOUNG (6–7 MONTHS OLD) GOOSE,
   4–5 KG (8–11 POUNDS)
1 LEMON, HALVED
1–1 1/2 TABLESPOONS SALT
1 TEASPOON WHITE PEPPER
2 TART APPLES
8–10 PITTED PRUNES
1 DL (1/2 CUP) CHICKEN STOCK

Sauce:
GOOSE GIBLETS
1 ONION
1 CARROT
2 TABLESPOONS ALL-PURPOSE FLOUR
2 DL (1 CUP) WATER
1 TEASPOON THYME
1 TEASPOON TOMATO PASTE
1 BAY LEAF
SALT AND PEPPER
1 DL (1/2 CUP) BLACKBERRIES
   OR RASPBERRIES
2 TABLESPOONS RED WINE VINEGAR
3 TABLESPOONS BUTTER

Remove the giblets and reserve for the sauce. Clean and rinse the goose both inside and out. Cut off the wing tips and reserve for the sauce. Dry the goose well with paper towels.

Preheat the oven to 175°C (350°F). Rub the goose, both inside and out, with the cut lemon, salt and pepper. Prick all over with a skewer, so the fat can render. Core the apples and cut into wedges. Stuff the goose with prunes and apples.

Sew or tie the goose with cotton string. Place on its side on a rack over an oven tray. Add the chicken stock to the pan and roast the goose for 30–40 minutes. Pour off fat as it accumulates (and use for frying potatoes). Turn the goose onto the other side and roast for 30–40 minutes more. Turn the goose breast up and roast for around 40 minutes more. A young goose should be done after around 2 1/2 hours.

Test if the meat is ready by poking a skewer into the thigh. If the juices run clear, it is done. Try to remove the goose from the oven around 10 minutes before it is finished cooking. Pour off as much fat as possible and pour the pan juices into the simmering stock for the sauce. Sprinkle the goose with salt and return it to the oven with the door open, so that the skin becomes dry and crunchy.

Sauce:
Prepare the sauce while the goose is roasting.

Chop the gizzard, neck, wing tips and heart into small pieces. Peel and chop the onion and carrot. Brown in goose fat. Sprinkle with flour and gradually add the water. Slowly heat to boiling. Add thyme, tomato paste, bay leaf, salt and pepper. Let the gravy simmer while the goose is roasting. Strain.

Add half of the pan juices to the goose stock. Heat to boiling, skimming well. Add berries and vinegar. Just before serving, whisk in the butter. Do not allow the sauce to boil after the butter has been added.

When the goose is ready, transfer to a cutting board and let rest for a few minutes. Remove the string. Cover the legs with foil. Carve out the breasts and slice on the diagonal. Cut off the legs and slice the thighs.

Serve the goose with potatoes, pickled red cabbage and Brussels sprouts along with sautéed apple halves filled with prunes.

If you want to serve Hasselback potatoes, see the recipe on page 24.

Apple cake
from Skåne

Skånsk äppelkaka

4 SERVINGS

125 G (4 1/2 OUNCES) ZWIEBACK
1/2 DL (1/4 CUP) BREADCRUMBS
1/2 DL (1/4 CUP) SUGAR
100 G (3 1/2 OUNCES) BUTTER
1 TABLESPOON CINNAMON
2 APPLES
1/2 DL (1/4 CUP) APPLESAUCE

VANILLA SAUCE (RECIPE PAGE 34)
    OR WHIPPED CREAM

Preheat the oven to 200 °C (400 °F).
Grate the zwieback into fine crumbs.
Sauté zwieback crumbs, breadcrumbs
and sugar in butter. Sprinkle with
cinnamon, combine and set aside.

Peel and core the apples and cut into
thin wedges. Mix with applesauce. Layer
the crumbs with the apples in 4 greased
individual forms or in an ovenproof
dish. Bake for 20 minutes.

Serve with vanilla sauce or whipped
cream

Crispbread

Most Swedes have eaten crispbread since they were children. In the olden days, flatbread was baked with a hole in the middle so it could be threaded onto a pole for storage. Sometime it was stored literally for years. The modern version of this bread and a particular brand of vodka are among Sweden's most successful exports today. An increased awareness of the benefits of eating whole grain and fiber-rich food has led to a comeback for crispbread even among the young. Crispbread is not just good for you, it also keeps well.

Crispbread

Knäckebröd

25 DISCS

1 DL (1/2 CUP) VEGETABLE OIL
2 DL (1 CUP) WATER
50 G (1 3/4 OUNCES) FRESH YEAST
1/2 TEASPOON SALT
1 1/2 TABLESPOONS ANISE SEED
1 1/2 TABLESPOONS FENNEL SEED
1 1/2 TABLESPOONS CARAWAY SEED
3 DL (1 1/2 CUPS) COARSE RYE FLOUR
2–3 DL (1 CUP) SIFTED RYE FLOUR
ALL-PURPOSE FLOUR FOR KNEADING

Pour the oil into a saucepan, add the water and heat to lukewarm, 37 °C (98 °F). Pour into a baking bowl, crumble in the yeast and stir in the spices and the coarse rye flour. Add only as much sifted rye flour as is necessary for the dough to stick together – it should be loose.

Preheat the oven to 225 °C (425 °F).

Turn the dough onto a well-floured baking board. Knead lightly and divide into 25 pieces of equal size. Roll each into a ball, then roll each with a textured rolling pin into a very thin round sheet. For a traditional look, cut a hole toward one end with a glass or round cookie cutter.

While you are rolling out the discs, heat a baking sheet in the oven. Place a disc on the sheet and bake in the center of the oven for 1–2 minutes. The vent (if there is one) should be open.

With a little practice, you should be able to roll out one disc in the time it takes for one to bake.

Advent

There are few places in the world as dark as Sweden in December, so it is only natural that celebrating Advent is typically Swedish. Advent means arrival and anticipation. Four Sundays before Christmas, we light the first candle on the four-armed candlestick in our window, and we invite friends home for glögg (in the beginning it was mulled wine) and gingerbread cookies. During this busy time, there are Christmas markets and Christmas displays in store windows. Nobel prizes are awarded and the world-renowned Swedish smorgasbord changes its name to Christmas table and sets the stage for some of the wildest employee parties of the year.

CHRISTER LINGSTRÖM:
"Gingerbread brings out the best in people" is an old Swedish saying. Gingerbread, which came to Stockholm in the 1500s, used to be considered medicine. It was thought to cure cholera, diarrhea, weakness and melancholy and to help digestion. Some of the spices in it are known as medicinal plants, so maybe there is something to that after all. Try eating gingerbread cookies with blue cheese – it's a delicacy you can serve year-round."

Advent glögg

Adventsglögg

1 BOTTLE REASONABLY PRICED RED WINE
  (75 CL/3 CUPS)
15 CARDAMOM SEEDS
1 CINNAMON STICK
1 CHUNK BITTER ORANGE PEEL OR
  1 TEASPOON GROUND BITTER
  ORANGE PEEL
1 CHUNK FRESH GINGER, 20 G
  (2/3 OUNCE), PEELED AND COARSELY
  CHOPPED
2 DL (3/4 CUP) SUGAR
RAISINS
ALMONDS

Combine wine, spices and sugar in a
saucepan. Let marinate for 1–2 hours.

Heat slowly to almost boiling. Strain.

Serve with raisins and almonds.

Blue cheese-walnut pie

Paj till glögg

20 SMALL SERVINGS

Swedes have been drinking glögg since
the days of Gustav Vasa. He even had
his own royal glöggmaker. Gustav Vasa
was crowned king on June 6, 1523 in
Strängnäs, so the tradition has nearly
five centuries of history behind it.

Pie crust:
3 DL (1 1/4 CUPS) ALL-PURPOSE FLOUR
1/2 DL (3 TABLESPOONS) SUGAR
1 TEASPOON GROUND CINNAMON
1 TEASPOON GROUND GINGER
1/2 TEASPOON GROUND CLOVES
150 G (5 OUNCES) BUTTER
2 TABLESPOONS WHIPPING CREAM

Filling:
150 G (5 OUNCES) BLUE CHEESE
100 G (3 1/2 OUNCES) WALNUTS
1 DL (1/2 CUP) RAISINS
2 EGGS
2 DL (1 CUP) WHIPPING CREAM

Combine all ingredients for the pie crust
by hand or pulse in a food processor.

Press into a loose-bottomed pie tin.
Cover and refrigerate for around an
hour.

Preheat the oven to 180°C (350°F).
Prick the pie crust with a fork. Bake in
the center of the oven for 15 minutes.

Grate the cheese and mix with the
nuts and raisins and sprinkle over the
pie crust. Whisk the eggs and cream
together and pour over the cheese
mixture.

Bake in the lower part of the oven for
30 minutes, until set. Serve lukewarm
with glögg.

Gingerbread with blue cheese cream and fresh figs

Pepparkaka med ädelost-crème och färska fikon

10 SERVINGS

150 G (5 OUNCES) KVIBILLE BLUE CHEESE
  OR OTHER BLUE CHEESE
1/2 DL (3 1/2 TABLESPOONS)
  CRÈME FRAICHE
10 GINGERBREAD COOKIES
2 FRESH FIGS, THINLY SLICED

Beat cheese and crème fraiche until
smooth. Spread on the cookies and top
with fig slices.

Serve with port, preferably vintage,
or glögg.

Recipe for gingerbread cookies
on page 86.

Lucia

The first person who saw the queen of light was a priest from Skåne. In 1764, he stayed overnight at a castle in Västergötland. When he awakened the next morning, he thought he had died and gone to heaven. The whole room was lit with candles, and beside his bed was an angel with wings and long hair who sang.

Although Swedes consider Lucia a very Swedish figure, we don't really know where she originated. Most sources say that she was a young Sicilian, who died a martyr's death in 304. Her fiancé accused her of giving her dowry to the poor, and eventually she was sentenced to death.

There are many legends surrounding Lucia, but we know for a fact that today's celebration of Lucia's day at schools and daycare centers with girls in white dresses with candle crowns, star boys and glitter originated on December 13, 1927, when a morning newspaper arranged a Lucia parade through Stockholm.

CHRISTER LINGSTRÖM:
"When the iron stove entered the Swedish kitchen during the 1800s, it became possible to bake saffron rolls at home. The best known saffron roll is the Lucia bun, also called the Lucia cat, which is served by Lucia early in the morning."

Lucia buns

Lussebullar

25 LARGE OR 50 SMALL

2 1/2 DL (1 CUP) MILK
1 1/2 DL (2/3 CUP) SUGAR
50 G (1 3/4 OUNCES) FRESH YEAST
12 DL (5 CUPS) ALL-PURPOSE FLOUR
200 G (7 OUNCES) SOFT UNSALTED BUTTER
2 G (1/2 TEASPOON) SAFFRON
1 TEASPOON GROUND CARDAMOM
1 EGG
2 TEASPOONS SALT
150 G (5 OUNCES) RAISINS OR
   MORE ACCORDING TO TASTE

For brushing:
1 EGG, LIGHTLY BEATEN

Heat the milk to 30 °C (98 °C), add the sugar and crumble in the yeast. Add all the remaining ingredients except for the raisins. Knead or use a mixer equipped with a dough hook for 10–15 minutes. Carefully knead in the raisins. They should not disintegrate.

Cover and let rise at room temperature for 30 minutes.

Divide the dough into 25 pieces (or 50, for small rolls). Roll into 15–20 cm (6–8 inch) lengths and twist the ends of both sides toward the middle in opposite directions to make a pinwheel or "Lucia cat". Press a raisin in the center of each coil.

Place the buns on a baking sheet lined with parchment paper (Note: place them far apart). Cover and let rise until double.

Preheat the oven to 220 °C (420 °F). Bake for around 5 minutes. Remove from the oven and brush with beaten egg. Return to the oven for 1 minute more.

Serve slightly warm with a glass of cold milk.

Christmas

Everyone has a dream about how Christmas should be. The favorite Swedish holiday should be as red as Santa's coat and green as the tree that has a place of honor in every home for the 20 days of the holiday. There aren't many places where Santa makes "house calls" as he does in Sweden. In most other countries, he is usually found at department stores. In the beginning, he was said to be German and called St. Nikolaus. In rural Sweden of old, people showed their generosity at Christmas. Everyone who helped out on the farm was paid at Christmas, even the grumpy, seldom seen little elf who took care of the animals. Servants got clothing, food, beer, candles and bread. No one was forgotten or allowed to leave the home without being offered something. No one wanted Christmas gifts in those days, because they were not really presents at all. Young people would knock on the door and then throw in a chunk of wood or a pig's foot wrapped in paper with a naughty verse (this is where Christmas rhymes originated). Then they would scatter.

CHRISTER LINGSTRÖM:
"I like a traditional Christmas. At Edsbacka Krog, we begin preparations in March. Don't even try to make a Christmas table like ours, with its 60 different dishes. Make 10 to 12. Christmas is supposed to be a holiday when the family can spend time together, not when you have to work all day long in the kitchen."

Gingerbread cookies
Pepparkakor

"Gingerbread brings out the best in people" is an old Swedish saying.

When gingerbread is in the oven, you can enjoy the aroma of bitter orange peel, ginger and cloves. Here is a recipe for simple, easy, crisp gingerbread cookies.

AROUND 60 COOKIES

2 DL (1 CUP) CORN OR SUGAR SYRUP
200 G (7 OUNCES) BUTTER
2 DL (3/4 CUP) BROWN SUGAR
2 TEASPOONS BAKING SODA
2 TEASPOONS GROUND CLOVES
1 TEASPOON GROUND BITTER ORANGE PEEL
1 TEASPOON GROUND GINGER
2 EGGS
1 LITER (4 1/4 CUPS) ALL-PURPOSE FLOUR

Heat syrup to boiling. Add butter and sugar and stir until mixture is cold. Add spices and eggs and then flour.

Many say that this dough should spend a week in the refrigerator, but a few days should do.

Preheat the oven to 200°C (400°F).

Roll the dough into a thin sheet. Cut out cookies with Christmas cookie cutters and place on a baking sheet lined with parchment paper. Bake in the center of the oven for 5–10 minutes depending on the thickness.

Serve with warm glögg (see recipe on page 82).

Dill and garlic marinated Baltic herring

Dill- och vitlöks-gravad strömming

4–6 SERVINGS

600 G (1 1/3 POUNDS) FRESH HERRING
   FILLETS

Brine:
5 DL (2 CUPS) WATER
1/2 DL (3 1/2 TABLESPOONS)
   24% VINEGAR CONCENTRATE
1 TABLESPOON SALT
DILL STALKS

Sauce:
200 G (7 OUNCES) FRESH DILL
1/2 DL (3 1/2 TABLESPOONS) 3% MILK
3 GARLIC CLOVES, CRUSHED
3 TABLESPOONS MAYONNAISE
2 DL (1 CUP) CRÈME FRAICHE
   OR SOUR CREAM
WHITE PEPPER

Rinse the fish in cold water. Combine water, vinegar and salt. (As a substitute for 24% vinegar concentrate and water, use 5 1/2 dl (2 1/4 cups) 5% vinegar.) Pluck the dill strands and reserve for the sauce. Coarsely chop the stalks and add them to the brine with the fish. Marinate the fish until the meat is white, 4–6 hours in the refrigerator. Drain the fillets and remove the skin.

Place the dill and milk in a food processor and puree. Press through a sieve. Combine dill liquid, garlic, mayonnaise and crème fraiche. Season with pepper. Fold into the herring and refrigerate until serving, preferably for 12–24 hours.

Garnish with dill sprigs.

Gravad lax (Marinated salmon)

Gravad lax

The Old Swedish word "grava" means grave and comes from the old usage of the word, meaning to bury containers of fish in a hole in the ground and let them ferment. This method of preparing fish has been around for a very long time, maybe even since the early Stone Age. To bury food as a means of preservation is still used in many places.

Does it really matter which kind of salt is used? It actually does. Mineral salt should not be used in recipes such as this. For "graving" of fish or meat, you should use regular salt without iodine, as iodized salt can leave an aftertaste.

"Gravad" fish should always be frozen for at least 48 hours, preferably longer, either before or after preparation.

6 SERVINGS

1 KG (2 1/4 POUNDS) BONELESS SALMON
   FILLETS, SKIN ON
1/2 DL (1/4 CUP) SUGAR
1/2 DL (1/4 CUP) SALT
1 TABLESPOON CRUSHED WHITE
   PEPPERCORNS
1 BUNCH DILL

Remove any small bones from the fish. Scrape the fillets carefully with a knife. Do not rinse in water.

Combine sugar, salt and pepper. Rinse the dill, drain and coarsely chop. Sprinkle a large piece of plastic wrap with a little of the sugar-salt mixture and some dill. Place one fish fillet, skin side down, on the plastic wrap. Sprinkle with the sugar-salt mixture and dill. Top with the other salmon fillet, skin side up, facing the other direction. The meaty sides face one another, and the thick end of one fillet lies against the thin end of the other. Sprinkle with the remaining sugar-salt mixture.

Wrap the plastic wrap around the fish to make a tight package. Place in a plastic bag and knot the end. Refrigerate for at least 24 hours, turning the package at least once.

Make the mustard sauce.

Scrape the dill and sugar-salt mixture from the salmon. Cut into thin, diagonal slices, pressing the knife against the skin as you cut.

Serve with mustard sauce, lemon wedges, toast and butter.

Mustard sauce

Senapssås

1/2 DL (1/4 CUP) SWEET SWEDISH
   MUSTARD
1–2 TABLESPOONS SUGAR
1/4 TEASPOON SALT
2 TABLESPOONS VINEGAR
1 DL (1/2 CUP) VEGETABLE OIL
1/2 DL (1/4 CUP) FINELY CHOPPED DILL

Mix together mustard, sugar, salt and vinegar. Whisk in the oil by the drop. The sauce should be thick and shiny. Stir in the dill. Taste and adjust seasoning, if necessary.

Red cabbage

Rödkål

4–6 SERVINGS

I HEAD RED CABBAGE (3/4–I KG)
   I 3/4–2 I/4 POUNDS
3–4 TART APPLES
I ONION
BUTTER
5 WHOLE CLOVES
3 ALLSPICE BERRIES
I TEASPOON SALT
2–3 TABLESPOONS VINEGAR
3 TABLESPOONS CURRANT JELLY
   OR BLACK CURRANT JUICE

Clean the cabbage and peel the apples.
Shred the cabbage and remove the
stalk. Core the apples. Peel the onion.
Cut the apples and onion into wedges.

Sauté cabbage and onion in butter in
a pot. Add the remaining ingredients.
Cover and let simmer for 40–50
minutes, stirring occasionally.

Serve with ham or pork ribs.

Christmas ham

Julskinka

I LIGHTLY SALTED HAM 2–6 KG
   (4 I/2–I3 POUNDS)

Most people buy their ham already
salted, but this recipe is for those who
want to salt their ham themselves.

Salting the Christmas ham:

Rubbing:
4 TABLESPOONS (I/4 CUP) SALT
2 TABLESPOONS SUGAR
I/2 TABLESPOON SALTPETER (OPTIONAL)

Brine:
5 LITERS (QUARTS) WATER
900 G (2 POUNDS) SALT, PREFERABLY
   WITHOUT IODINE, AS IT CAN LEAVE AN
AFTERTASTE
2 TABLESPOONS SUGAR
I/2 TABLESPOON SALTPETER (OPTIONAL)

Combine ingredients for rubbing and
rub them thoroughly all over the ham.
Double the amount for a very large ham
(7–8 kg /15–17 pounds).

Combine ingredients for the brine. Add
saltpeter, if desired. The ham will keep
longer and the color will be redder. If
you use too much saltpeter, the ham
can be hard. Heat the brine to boiling.
Skim well and let it cool. Pour over the
ham. It should cover well. Turn the ham
occasionally and store in a cold place.
A large ham (over 6 kg/13 pounds)
should soak in brine for around 3
weeks, a smaller ham (3–4 kg/6 1/2–
9 pounds) for around two weeks. Before
cooking, soak the ham in cold water
for two hours if it is to be boiled,
for 15 hours if it is to be baked.

Baked ham:
Preheat the oven to 175°C (350°F).
Wrap the ham in aluminum foil and
bake in an ovenproof dish or oven tray.
Use a dish or tray with high sides,
because of the cooking liquid.

Insert a meat thermometer through the
foil into the thickest part of the ham.
Bake until it reaches 70°C (160°F).
The ham can be baked without foil in
a 125°C (250°F) oven. A meat thermometer is absolutely necessary for
preparing ham to the correct degree of
doneness. At 70°C (160°F), it is juicy
and should be removed from the oven
and cooled relatively quickly. Save the
cooking juices.

Grill the ham, and the lovely aroma will
spread through the kitchen. It's so good
that you have to eat a slice before it
cools.

Grilling the ham:
2 EGG YOLKS
4 TABLESPOONS (I/4 CUP) SWEDISH
   MUSTARD
I TEASPOON POTATO STARCH (OPTIONAL)
I I/2–2 DL (3/4 CUP) BREADCRUMBS

Preheat the oven grill to 200°C (400°F).

Combine egg yolks and mustard. Add
potato starch to thicken the mixture,
if desired. Spread over the ham and sift
over the crumbs.

Grill the ham in the center of the oven
for 10–11 minutes, until the crumbs are
golden. Turn the ham several times for
an even color.

Keep an eye on the grill. Sometimes
it goes more quickly than you think,
according to a friend who now sits on a
stool facing the oven window after one
Christmas when he burned the ham.

Jansson's temptation

Janssons frestelse

4 SERVINGS

8–10 POTATOES
2 ONIONS
I SMALL LEEK
2 TABLESPOONS BUTTER
20 ANCHOVY FILLETS
I DL (1/2 CUP) MILK
2 DL (I CUP) WHIPPING CREAM
BUTTER

Preheat the oven to 200 °C (400 °F).

Peel the potatoes and cut into match-
stick pieces around 5 cm (2 inches)
long. Peel and thinly slice the onion.
Clean and shred the leek. Sauté onion
and leek in butter until tender. Drain
the anchovies, reserving the brine.
Layer potatoes, onion and anchovies in
a greased ovenproof dish, beginning and
ending with potatoes. Combine the
milk, cream and 2–3 tablespoons
anchovy brine. Pour over the potato
mixture. Dot with butter.

Bake in the center of the oven for
around 45 minutes. Cover with foil
toward the end, if the top becomes too
brown.

Serve with crispbread, butter and
cheese.

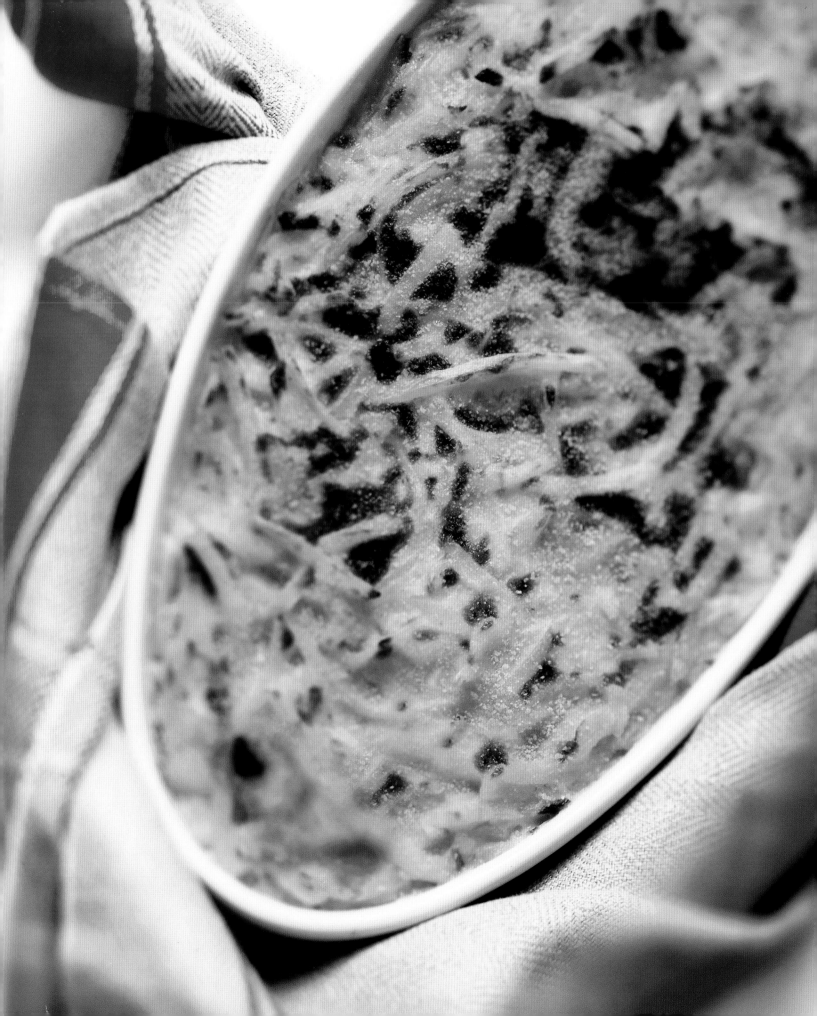

Ice chocolate
with nuts, raisins
and orange

Ischoklad med nötter, russin
och smak av apelsin

50–60 PIECES

A delicious and easy treat that can be
flavored in any way you wish.

225 G (8 OUNCES) SEMI-SWEET CHOCOLATE
200 G (7 OUNCES) COCONUT FAT
RAISINS
NUTS
CHOPPED CANDIED ORANGE PEEL

Melt the chocolate and coconut fat
together over low heat or in a micro-
wave oven. Stir until completely melted
and blended.

Stir the raisins, nuts and orange peel
into the chocolate mixture. Spoon into
small foil cups.

Refrigerate until the chocolate sets.

Recipes

Christer thanks for help at the stove:
Fredrik Eagle Pettersson and Viktor Lejon

Thanks for lending us props:
Nils Olsson Hemslöjd AB
Cervera Regeringsgatan
Boda Nova
Höganäs
Orrefors/Kosta Boda
Klässbols Linneväveri
Rörstrand
Design House Stockholm
Nittsjö Keramik
Gustavsberg

For their great help in Dalarna, we thanks:
Bengt and Britt-Marie Petersson
and Christina Böhlmark,
Land Alice Gustavsson,
Celine and Kristin Hansson,
Lucia Sanna Holm

www.formapg.se/bok

Forma Publishing Group AB is milieu-certified
according to ISO 14001

English translation and recipe adaptation:
Melody Favish
Book concept, project leader and prop manager:
Ingela Holm
Editor: Gunilla Wagner
Recipes and arrangements: Christer Lingström
Text: Lennart Häger
Photographer: Bruno Ehrs
Photo assistant: Thomas Thelin
Graphic design: Kjell Benettsson
Creative consultant: Pelle Holm
Repro: Done
Printed by Rotolito Lombarda SpA, Italy 2008

ISBN 978-91-534-2990-6